"SHESOAR"

21 Days of Empowering Affirmations & Self-Reflection

Angela Daniel

Unless otherwise indicated, all Scripture quotations are taken from The Holy Bible, New International Version, NIV.

Cover Design by SheSoar Desizns
shesoardesizns@gmail.com

SheSoar 21 Days of Empowering Affirmations & Self-Reflection

ISBN: 9798879882339

DEDICATION

I dedicate this book to the unwavering spirit that lives within you and seeks light even in the darkest times.

Acknowledgments

I want to thank my mom, Shirley Cruise. You have shown me what power, resilience and strength look like in the face of adversity. When the going got rough you never backed away, you faced it head-on and made it work for us. To my dad Robert Daniel who has left this earthly home to live in his heavenly home. Thank you for living out your strength before me.

To my children, Brittni, Ma'Chael, and Me'Chellia. Thank you for allowing me to parent you the best I could. Thank you for your patience, understanding, and never-ending love. You made me the strong, resilient woman I am today. To my grandbabies, Jessiah, Kaydin, Aubree, Amiah, and Keith Jr. Nene never knew love like this until she met you. Thank you for allowing me to show you strength, love, and resilience amid a world full of uncertainty. To my sister Doris, thank you for your encouraging words and push.

Casey, thank you for your patience, understanding, and push. You see in me what I do not see in myself and I'm grateful that we are walking through life together.

To Nicole, my friend and prayer warrior. You have always been a listening ear and my reminder of strength in the midst of challenges. I thank you with my whole heart.

Thanks to my spiritual leaders and coaches. It's because of you I was able to come into reality that I'm worthy of every good and perfect gift from God. Thank you for giving me your time, talent, and words of encouragement reminding me that I am fearfully and wonderfully made.

TABLE OF CONTENTS

Introduction 4

Day 1: Unstoppable Strength.. 6

Day 2: Embracing Growth.. 12

Day 3: Confidence Unleashed.. 18

Day 4: Vision Renewed.. 24

Day 5: Dreams to Reality... 30

Day 6: Becoming My Best.. 36

Day 7: Unstoppable Capability.. 42

Day 8: Embracing Inner Kindness and Worth............................ 48

Day 9: United Journey.. 54

Day 10: Beyond Fear.. 60

Day 11: Destined for Greatness....................................... 66

Day 12: Faith Unshaken... 72

Day 13: Clarity Unveiled... 78

Day 14: Embracing Peaceful Thoughts.................................. 84

Day 15: Present Beauty... 90

Day 16: Letting Go of Fear to Shine Brightly......................... 96

Day 17: Making Choices for a Healthy Me.............................. 102

Day 18: Letting Go of Stress with Every Breath....................... 108

Day 19: Choosing Compassion.. 114

Day 20: Surrendering to Guidance..................................... 120

Day 21: Stepping Stones to Self...................................... 126

Closing 131
About Author..132

Introduction

"My mission for "SheSoar" 21 days of empowering your being affirmations and self-reflection is to create a sacred space within these pages of where words of empowerment, positivity, and self-reflection come together. I hope to inspire transformation by using affirmations to encourage a journey of self-discovery, growth, and empowerment.

The name "SheSoar" emphasizes the feminine experience. The word "Soar" suggests a journey of rising, climbing, and reaching new heights, which represents personal and professional growth.

This journal serves as a compass, guiding you toward your full potential, fostering resilience, and igniting a deep feeling of well-being. With each written affirmation, I hope to uplift spirits, cultivate self-love, and catalyze transformations to a more fulfilled and purpose-driven life for you."

DAY 1

"UNSTOPPABLE STRENGTH"

"I am a powerful and resilient woman; I can overcome any challenge that might come my way"

EMPOWER YOUR BEING

"I declare that I am *resilient* and *strong* in the face of adversity. I am a strong woman who can confidently approach any issue that presents a chance for personal development. I have faith that I can overcome any hardship and come out stronger. My path shows my tenacity, and I will never abandon my pursuit of happiness and success. I am a tough force to be reckoned with, and I am proud of the strong, independent woman I am becoming."

SELF-REFLECTION QUESTIONS

1. How can I celebrate and acknowledge my big and small victories as evidence of my capability to overcome challenges?

___

___

___

2. Are there areas of my life where I may underestimate my strength and capabilities? How can I shift that belief?

___

___

___

3. What self-care practices can I incorporate to nurture and strengthen my sense of power and resilience?

___

___

___

PRAYER

Lord, thank you for guiding me through life's difficulties. I believe that with you in my life, I can do anything, no matter how big or small.

DAY 2

"EMBRACING GROWTH"

"I am on a transformative journey, embracing each day as an opportunity for growth and self-discovery."

EMPOWER YOUR BEING

"I declare that with each step I take, I am confidently and purposefully moving toward my full potential. I am a shining example of empowerment, facing my journey with courage, resilience, and unwavering resolve. I am destined to become the empowered woman I was born to be, and I am excited about the transformative power of this evolution in every aspect of my life."

SELF-REFLECTION QUESTIONS

1. What specific actions or habits am I currently engaging in that align with my vision of confidently stepping into my fullest potential and becoming an empowered woman?

____

____

____

2. In what ways have I overcome challenges or obstacles on my journey toward empowerment, and how can I use these experiences for continued growth and resilience?

____

____

____

3. What limiting beliefs or self-doubts may be hindering my progress in confidently stepping into my fullest potential, and how can I actively work to reframe or overcome them?

____

____

____

PRAYER

As I embark on this transformative journey, I open my heart to the opportunities that each day brings. Grant me the strength to embrace growth and self-discovery with courage and humility. Please fill me with gratitude for the lessons, both big and small, that shaped my journey. May I find joy in self-discovery and celebrate the progress I make each day.

Amen

DAY 3

“CONFIDENT UNLEASHED”

"I release self-doubt and replace it with unwavering confidence. I trust in my abilities, and I believe in my unique talents. Today, I step boldly into my power."

EMPOWER YOUR BEING

"I declare a powerful shift within myself. I release the grip of self-doubt and step into the brilliance of my potential. With unwavering confidence, I acknowledge the unique strengths within me. I stand tall, embracing my worth, and affirming that my voice matters. I am no longer a prisoner of doubt, I am the architect of my destinies, shaping a future fueled by self-assurance, resilience, and the unwavering belief that I can achieve greatness."

SELF-REFLECTION QUESTIONS

1. What specific situations trigger feelings of self-doubt for me?

____

____

____

2. How have past experiences shaped my beliefs about myself?

____

____

____

3. What evidence exists to challenge my self-doubt?

____

____

____

PRAYER

Heavenly Father,

I release self-doubt from my being and invite unwavering confidence to fill my spirit. I have faith in my abilities and believe in my unique abilities. Today, I step boldly into my power, knowing that I am capable and deserving.

Amen

DAY 4

"VISION RENEWED"

"I see the new purpose of my life"

EMPOWER YOUR BEING

"It is now time to act on this new purpose. I am grateful for all the things I have learned so far in my life. I am happy that my life has become a thing of beauty. Just as the lotus flower rises through the muck toward the light, I am now appearing in the light of my legacy. I see now what was unclear to me before. I have clarity of purpose."

SELF-REFLECTION QUESTIONS

1. What can I do to see my purpose more clearly?

   ____

   ____

   ____

2. What do I need to journal now that will be useful for my legacy?

   ____

   ____

   ____

3. What is my next action step?

   ____

   ____

   ____

PRAYER

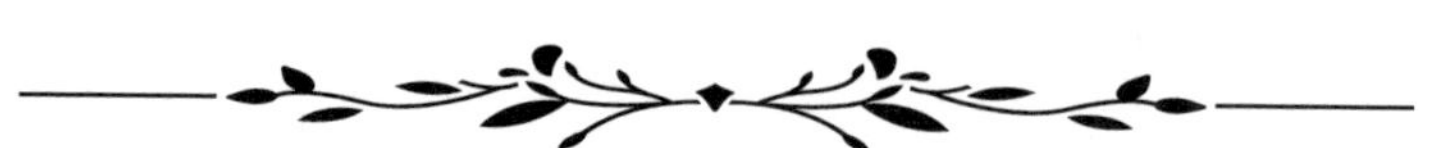

I acknowledge the dawning of a new purpose in my life, a purpose divinely woven into the fabric of my being. Fill my days with purposeful actions, my words with kindness, and my heart with gratitude. May I be a beacon of inspiration to others, reflecting the love and purpose you have bestowed upon me. I surrender my old self to embrace the new purpose you have revealed. With gratitude and trust, I walk this path knowing that your divine guidance lights the way.

Amen.

DAY 5

"DREAMS TO REALITY"

"My dreams are more than simply wishes; they are attainable goals. I pledge to make my ideas a reality, flying to new heights of achievement with dedication and purpose."

EMPOWER YOUR BEING

Jeremiah 29:11 (NIV): "For I know the plans I have for you, declares the Lord, plans for welfare and not for evil, to give you a future and a hope."

"*In* the pursuit of my dreams and aspirations, I declare that my path is guided by divine purpose. I trust in the plans that the Lord has for me, confident that every step I take aligns with His greater design. My dreams are not just personal desires; they are part of a larger, purposeful journey orchestrated by the Creator. As I move forward, I am open to divine guidance, knowing that my aspirations are intricately woven into the beautiful tapestry of God's plan for my life. With faith as my compass, I navigate toward a future filled with purpose, impact, and the fulfillment of His divine intentions for me"

SELF-REFLECTION QUESTIONS

1. In what ways am I consciously looking for and acknowledging divine guidance as I navigate this journey?

____

____

____

2. How can I deepen my connection with the spiritual aspect of my aspirations, allowing divine purpose to shape not only the destination but also the journey itself?

____

____

____

3. What steps can I take to further align my goals with the greater purpose that God has for me? As I reflect on my dreams, am I open to adjusting my path in response to the divine nudges and insights that may be guiding me?

____

____

____

PRAYER

Grant me the clarity to see the path that leads to the realization of my dreams. Kindle the flame of dedication within my heart, a flame that will illuminate even the darkest corners of doubt. May I recognize the potential within my ideas and the strength to transform them into tangible achievements? Guide my actions, thoughts, and decisions toward the manifestation of my dreams. May my endeavors not only serve my growth but also inspire and uplift those around me. Help me cultivate a spirit of discipline and focus, turning each day into a step closer to the fulfillment of my aspirations.

Amen

DAY 6

"BECOMING MY BEST"

"I am proud of the person I am becoming."

EMPOWER YOUR BEING

"I am proud of the person I am becoming, embracing growth, learning, and positive transformation on this incredible journey of self-discovery and personal development. "With every success I achieve, I feel an enormous sense of pride. I understand that each victory is just a small part of my journey to success. While I understand that I have made mistakes and errors in the past, I also appreciate these. I embrace them and cherish them, seeing them for the learning opportunities that they truly were. There are no obstacles that can block my path - I am always moving forward."

SELF-REFLECTION QUESTIONS

1. In what ways have my values and beliefs evolved positively, and how do they align with the person I aspire to be?

____

____

____

2. How do I actively engage in self-care and self-love to nurture my well-being and contribute to my overall sense of pride?

____

____

____

3. What steps can I take to continue evolving and growing into the person I aspire to be while supporting a sense of humility and openness to further development?

____

____

____

PRAYER

I come before you with gratitude for the journey of self-discovery and growth. Thank you for guiding me on the path of becoming the person I am proud to be. Grant me the strength to continue embracing change, the wisdom to learn from every experience, and the courage to face challenges with resilience. As I reflect on my journey, I acknowledge the progress I have made and the lessons I have learned. Fill my heart with gratitude for the person I am becoming and help me stay true to my values and purpose. May your light illuminate my path, and may I continue to evolve into the best version of myself. I am grateful for your constant presence and the transformative power of self-love.

Amen

DAY 7

"UNSTOPPABLE CAPABILITY"

"I am capable of handling anything. I act and set myself up for success."

EMPOWER YOUR BEING

"I can get through anything if I believe it will happen. I can manage all situations that come my way and focus on my approach to each case, knowing that I can manifest success. I complete the challenges I take on. If I begin to doubt myself or my ability to manage a challenge, I remind myself that I can do it. I say aloud. "Yes, I know that I can get through this." I function as though I already have made it happen. I let go of the question and go ahead and do it. And if I fail, I accept failure and learn to get back up again."

SELF-REFLECTION QUESTIONS

1. What could I say to convince myself that I can get through anything?

___

___

___

2. How have I overcome adversity in the past?

___

___

___

3. In which ways does building resilience improve my relationships?

___

___

___

PRAYER

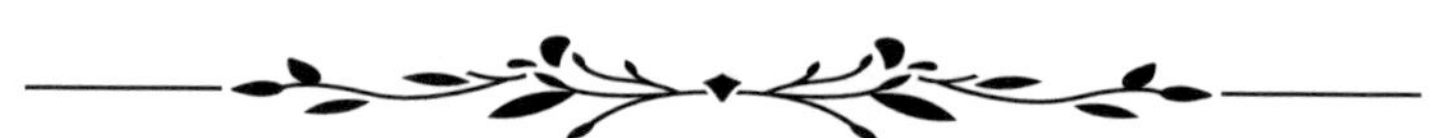

I stand before you with a heart filled with gratitude for the strength and resilience you've bestowed upon me. I affirm that I am capable of handling anything that comes my way. With your guidance, I find the courage to face challenges and the wisdom to overcome obstacles. I trust in your divine support as I set myself up for success. Help me cultivate the habits and mindset that lead to growth and achievement. Thank you for the opportunities before me, and may I make the most of them with confidence and gratitude.

Amen

DAY 8

"EMBRACING INNER KINDNESS AND WORTH"

"I treat myself with the same love and kindness I offer to others. I am a treasure deserving of my affection. Today, I commit to nurturing a deep and genuine love for myself."

EMPOWER YOUR BEING

"I declare that I am worthy of love and kindness. I choose to embrace and appreciate myself, acknowledging my strengths and accepting my imperfections. In doing so, I am better equipped to extend genuine love and compassion to others. I commit to treating myself with the same care and respect that I offer to those around me. May my actions and words reflect the love that flows within me, creating a positive and uplifting environment for myself and others. Today, I choose love as my guiding principle, fostering connections and spreading joy in every interaction."

SELF-REFLECTION QUESTIONS

1. What does self-love mean to me?

____

____

____

2. How do I prioritize self-care in my daily routine?

____

____

____

3. In what ways do I show love and kindness to others?

____

____

____

PRAYER

I come to you with a heart open to love, both for others and, most importantly, for myself. I acknowledge that I am a treasure deserving of my affection, just as much as anyone else. Help me cultivate a deep and genuine love for myself, recognize my worth, and embrace the unique qualities that make me who I am. Allow me to release any self-critical thoughts and replace them with affirmations of love and acceptance. Thank you for the grace to love me unconditionally and for the strength to carry this commitment forward.

Amen

DAY 9

"UNITED JOURNEY"

"I am not alone in my journey; I am surrounded by the strength of those who support and uplift me."

EMPOWER YOUR BEING

"I declare that I am not alone on my journey. I am surrounded by unseen forces of support, love, and encouragement. In every step I take, I am accompanied by the collective strength of those who believe in me. The universe conspires in my favor, and I am connected to a web of support that uplifts and guides me through every challenge. I embrace the comforting truth that I am never truly alone, for the energy of connection and encouragement is a constant companion on my path."

SELF-REFLECTION QUESTIONS

1. In what ways have others supported and encouraged me during challenging times?

____

____

____

2. How might sharing my story contribute to a sense of collective understanding and shared journeys?

____

____

____

3. Do I feel a sense of connection with something beyond the physical, such as a higher power, nature, or a sense of purpose?

____

____

____

PRAYER

I come before you with a heart full of appreciation for the connections that surround me. Thank you for the gift of companionship and the relationships that nurture my spirit. I am grateful for the friends, family, and kindred souls who walk alongside me, providing strength and encouragement when I need it most. Thank you for the blessings of community, and may I always be mindful of the interconnectedness that makes this journey richer.

Amen.

DAY 10

“BEYOND FEAR”

"I am stronger than my fears, and I confidently face challenges with resilience."

EMPOWER YOUR BEING

"*I* declare that challenges are my stepping stones to growth and success. I confront my fears knowing that each obstacle is an opportunity for transformation and personal empowerment in my journey. "I declare, as it is written in Philippians 4:13, that I can do all things through Christ who strengthens me. In the face of challenges, I am not overcome by fear, for I trust in His guidance and draw upon His strength, facing each obstacle with unwavering resilience and faith in His divine plan for my life."

SELF-REFLECTION QUESTIONS

1. How have these fears affected my confidence and decision-making?

____

____

____

2. Are there any limiting beliefs about my abilities that contribute to my fears? How can I challenge and reframe these beliefs?

____

____

____

3. In what ways can I practice self-compassion and self-care to build a solid foundation for facing challenges with resilience?

____

____

____

PRAYER

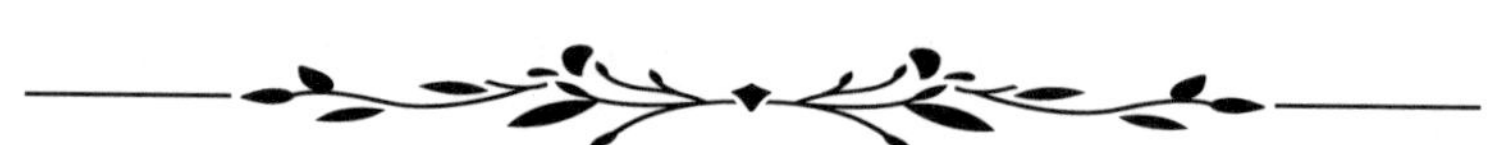

Lord, Grant me the strength to face my fears with courage and resilience. Help me believe in my inner strength and capabilities. May I find confidence in the face of challenges, knowing that I am stronger than my fears. Guide me through moments of doubt and fill my heart with the assurance that I can overcome any obstacle in my path. Thank you for the courage and resilience you instilled in me.

Amen.

DAY 11

"DESTINED FOR GREATNESS"

"I am worthy of success and deserving of all the good things life has to offer."

EMPOWER YOUR BEING

"I declare my commitment to nurturing unshakeable confidence within myself. I embrace my unique qualities, acknowledging that they contribute to my inherent worth. I stand tall in the face of challenges, recognizing them as opportunities for growth. I celebrate my achievements, both big and small, and affirm that I am deserving of success. With unwavering self-love and the support of my community, I boldly walk the path of confidence, inspiring others to do the same. I am a beacon of empowerment, illuminating the way for women to rise, thrive, and exude the radiance of unapologetic confidence."

SELF-REFLECTION QUESTIONS

1. In which areas of my life do I feel the most confident, and what factors contribute to that confidence?

____

____

____

2. What ways can I practice self-compassion and nurture my self-esteem daily?

____

____

____

3. How do my self-talk and inner dialogue impact my confidence, and what changes can I make to promote positive self-affirmation?

____

____

____

PRAYER

I humbly come before you, recognizing my worthiness of success and all the blessings life has to offer. May your guidance illuminate my path, helping me to seize opportunities and navigate challenges with grace. Grant me the strength to believe in my capabilities and the deserving nature of the good things that come my way. Thank you for the abundant blessings that unfold in my life.

DAY 12

"FAITH UNSHAKEN"

---

*"With unwavering faith,
I can ask for what I need
knowing that the Lord
will provide."*

EMPOWER YOUR BEING

"*I* declare with unwavering faith that I can confidently ask for what I need, trusting fully in the Lord's provision. I believe that through my faith, paths will open, and the resources I need will be provided according to His perfect plan and timing. I stand firm in this belief, knowing that my faith is the foundation of my journey, and the Lord is my guide. I am grateful for the abundance and blessings that flow into my life, knowing they are a testament to the Lord's endless generosity and love."

SELF-REFLECTION QUESTIONS

1. How can *PRAYER* strengthen my faith, particularly when asking for what I need? Do I feel a stronger connection with the Lord during these moments, and how does this improve my overall well-being?

____

____

____

2. In what ways does my unwavering faith help shape my view on life's challenges? How does it shape my reaction to situations where the outcome is uncertain?

____

____

____

3. What are the needs in my life that I should take to God in PRAYER, and how do they differ from my wants/desires? What role does my faith play in this distinction?

____

____

____

PRAYER

I come before you today during life's uncertainties. Help me to trust You completely, knowing that Your plans for me are perfect and right. I pray for Your comfort in my times of weakness. Remind me that I am never alone, for You are with me always. Your presence is my comfort, and Your promises give me hope. In moments of weakness.

Amen

DAY 13

"CLARITY UNVEILED"

"I release mental clutter and welcome clarity into my thoughts."

EMPOWER YOUR BEING

"I release the burdens of mental clutter that weigh heavy on my mind. I declare that I am free from the chains of confusion and doubt. As it is written in Philippians 4:7, 'And the peace of God, which transcends all understanding, will guard your hearts and your minds in Christ Jesus,' I invite the peace of God to guard my thoughts and grant me clarity. I cast away every anxious thought, for it is written in 1 Peter 5:7, 'Cast all your anxiety on him because he cares for you.' I choose to trust in the Lord with all my heart, as instructed in Proverbs 3:5-6, 'Trust in the Lord with all your heart and lean not on your understanding; in all your ways submit to him, and he will make your paths straight.' I welcome the clarity that comes from seeking God's wisdom, and I trust that He will guide my thoughts and actions."

SELF-REFLECTION QUESTIONS

1. In what areas of my life can I simplify and declutter to create mental space?

____

____

____

2. How do I prioritize and organize my daily tasks and responsibilities?

____

____

____

3. What thoughts or beliefs contribute to mental clutter in my mind?

____

____

____

PRAYER

Father, I surrender to the mental clutter that weighs down my thoughts. Grant me the wisdom to discern and focus on what truly matters. May my thoughts be clear, guided by purpose and understanding, leading me to a path of inner peace.

Amen

DAY 14

"EMBRACING PEACEFUL THOUGHTS"

"I cleanse my thoughts and embrace calm clarity with every breath."

EMPOWER YOUR BEING

"As I breathe in the life-giving air that the Creator has graciously provided, I release all mental clutter and welcome the peace that surpasses understanding. With each inhalation, I draw in clarity, and with each exhalation, I release any thoughts that do not serve my well-being. In the rhythm of my breath, I align with the divine order, trusting in the promise of Psalm 46:10, 'Be still, and know that I am God.' I declare that my mind is a sanctuary of calm and clarity, a sacred space where I am attuned to the wisdom of the universe. May each breath be a reminder of the divine presence within me, bringing tranquility and clarity to every aspect of my being."

SELF-REFLECTION QUESTIONS

1. What mental habits or patterns can I release with each exhalation to create more mental space?

 ____

 ____

 ____

2. How can I incorporate mindful breathing into my daily routine?

 ____

 ____

 ____

3. What thoughts or emotions arise when I intentionally focus on my breath?

 ____

 ____

 ____

PRAYER

Lord may my mind be at peace,
and may this serenity guide my
actions and decisions.

In Jesus Name,

Amen

DAY 15

"PRESENT BEAUTY "

"Each day, I embrace the beauty of the present moment, finding peace and purpose amid life's challenges."

EMPOWER YOUR BEING

"I can do all things through Christ who strengthens me. In times of uncertainty and challenge, I rest in the assurance that God's peace, which surpasses all understanding, guards my heart and mind. My purpose is anchored in His divine plan, and I trust that every obstacle is an opportunity for His glory to shine through me. With faith, I navigate through challenges, knowing that God's grace is sufficient, and His power is made perfect in my weakness. I am a vessel of peace and purpose, grounded in the love and promises of my Savior, Jesus Christ."

SELF-REFLECTION QUESTIONS

1. How can you reframe your perspective to see challenges as a means of discovering your strengths and deepening your understanding of yourself?

____

____

____

2. Identify the areas of your life that align with your purpose. How can you prioritize these aspects, even in the face of challenges?

____

____

____

3. Reflect on the principles and values that guide your life. How do these beliefs contribute to your sense of purpose and provide a foundation for inner peace during challenges?

____

____

____

PRAYER

Lord, grant me the strength to find peace and purpose amid life's challenges. Guide my heart and mind to appreciate the gifts of each moment, and may I be a source of encouragement and positivity to others. Help me teach and impact those around me with love, kindness, and understanding.

DAY 16

"LETTING GO OF FEAR TO SHINE BRIGHTLY"

"I choose joy over fear and let go of anything that dims my light."

EMPOWER YOUR BEING

"I am committed to choosing joy over fear in every aspect of my life. I recognize that fear may arise, but I consciously choose to let it go. I release any thoughts, beliefs, or situations that dim my light and hinder my happiness. I embrace the radiant energy within me and allow it to shine brightly. Today and every day, I affirm my power to choose joy, knowing that it not only brightens my path but also illuminates the way for others. I am a beacon of positivity, and my light is unstoppable."

SELF-REFLECTION QUESTIONS

1. How does fear impact my overall sense of joy and well-being?

____

____

____

2. What steps can I take to consciously choose joy in challenging situations?

____

____

____

3. In what ways can I let go of negativity and things that dim my light?

____

____

____

PRAYER

I release a shadow that may dim the light within me. Grant me the strength to let go of the worries and embrace the abundance of joy that surrounds me. Guide me to see the beauty in each day and find gratitude in every circumstance. Lord, I trust in your divine wisdom to lead me toward a path filled with positivity, love, and the unwavering light of joy. Thank you for the strength to release what no longer serves me and for the grace to welcome joy in my heart.

DAY 17

"MAKING CHOICES FOR A HEALTHY ME"

"My well-being is a priority, and I make choices that support my overall health."

EMPOWER YOUR BEING

"I declare that my well-being is of utmost importance in my life. I consciously and consistently make choices that contribute to my physical, mental, and emotional health. Each decision I make aligns with the nourishment and care my body, mind, and soul deserve. I am committed to cultivating a lifestyle that supports my overall well-being, allowing me to thrive and experience a fulfilling and healthy life."

SELF-REFLECTION QUESTIONS

1. In what areas of my life can I make more intentional choices to enhance my overall health and well-being?

____

____

____

2. What specific choices have I made recently that align with prioritizing my well-being?

____

____

____

3. How can I create a supportive environment that encourages and sustains my commitment to prioritizing my well-being?

____

____

____

PRAYER

I am grateful for the gift of life and the opportunity to prioritize my well-being. Today, I affirm that my health is a priority, and I choose to make decisions that nourish my body, mind, and spirit. Guide me in making choices that support my overall health and lead me toward a balanced and fulfilling life. May I be open to the wisdom within and around me?

DAY 18

“LETTING GO OF STRESS WITH EVERY BREATH"

"With every inhale, I welcome peace, and with every exhale, I let go of stress."

EMPOWER YOUR BEING

"In this sacred moment of breath, I declare my commitment to inviting peace into the depths of my being with every inhalation. As I draw in the life force around me, I embrace tranquility, allowing it to fill every cell of my body. Simultaneously, with each exhale, I release the grip of stress and tension that may have taken residence within me. I declare that my breath is a powerful instrument of renewal, a rhythmic dance between serenity and liberation. Today and always, I affirm my choice to breathe in peace and exhale stress, cultivating a harmonious existence within myself."

SELF-REFLECTION QUESTIONS

1. In what areas of my life do I currently experience stress, and how can I use my breath to release and let go of that stress during each exhale?

   ____

   ____

   ____

2. What physical sensations accompany the inhalation of peace, and how can I focus on those sensations to deepen my sense of calmness?

   ____

   ____

   ____

3. Are there specific thoughts or emotions that tend to arise during my exhalations, and how can I consciously let go of any negativity or stress associated with them?

   ____

   ____

   ____

PRAYER

Dear Father,

I consciously choose to align my breath with the rhythm of peace. I welcome the serene calmness that peace brings. With every exhale I release the grip of stress and I surrender to any tension or worry. I trust that as I let go, I make space for peace to expand within me.

DAY 19

"CHOOSING COMPASSION"

"I choose compassion in thought, speech, and behavior to create a peaceful atmosphere."

EMPOWER YOUR BEING

"I declare that from this moment forward, I consciously choose kindness in every thought, word, and action. My commitment to kindness is unwavering, and I am dedicated to creating a harmonious environment wherever I go. I understand the transformative power of my choices, and I embrace the responsibility to contribute positively to the world. Through intentional acts of kindness, I am a catalyst for harmony, fostering connections, understanding, and love. Today and every day, I affirm my role in shaping a compassionate and uplifting atmosphere, knowing that my commitment to kindness has a ripple effect that touches the hearts of others and contributes to the greater good. I am a beacon of positivity, and through my actions, I weave a tapestry of harmony in the fabric of the world around me."

SELF-REFLECTION QUESTIONS

1. What intentional acts of kindness have I engaged in recently, and how have they influenced the well-being of those around me?

___

___

___

2. Am I mindful of the language I use, ensuring that my words are uplifting and considerate?

___

___

___

3. What steps am I taking to continuously grow in my ability to choose kindness, not only in favorable circumstances but also in more challenging moments?

___

___

___

PRAYER

Father, allow my thoughts to be filled with compassion and empathy, my words to be soothing and kind, and my actions to reflect the softness of a caring heart. Help me to recognize the humanity in others so that I may comprehend their difficulties and respond with love and compassion. Thank you for your spiritual wisdom in choosing compassion in my thoughts, words, and actions.

DAY 20

"SURRENDERING TO GUIDANCE"

"I surrender my worries to God, knowing that His guidance will always lead me to the best outcomes."

EMPOWER YOUR BEING

"I chose to make a firm declaration: I give my troubles to God. This deliberate act of release is not an admission of defeat, but rather a brave embracing of trust. With each weight given to God, I find comfort in the unshakeable assurance that His wisdom is beyond my comprehension and will always lead me to the best results. This submission demonstrates my strength, an understanding that genuine power comes from letting go and letting God's plan develop. I surrender fear and worry in the arms of faith, leaving a place for the transformational calm that comes from trusting in the divine order of things. I manage the ebbs and flows of life with confidence, led by the unseen hand."

SELF-REFLECTION QUESTIONS

1. How does holding onto these worries affect my mental and emotional well-being?

____

____

____

2. What scriptures, prayers, or spiritual practices resonate with me in times of worry?

____

____

____

3. How can I cultivate a mindset of trust and faith in God's plan, especially when faced with uncertainty?

____

____

____

PRAYER

Dear Heavenly Father, in this moment of communion, I come before You with a humble heart, ready to surrender my worries into Your loving hands. I acknowledge that Your wisdom surpasses my understanding, and I place my trust in Your divine guidance. I surrender the weight of my anxieties, fears, and uncertainties, knowing that You are the ultimate orchestrator of my life's journey. As I release these burdens, I invite Your presence to fill the void with the soothing balm of peace and assurance.

DAY 21

STEPPING STONES TO SELF"

"I surrender to the flow of life, trusting that every experience is a stepping stone to my higher self."

EMPOWER YOUR BEING

"I declare my conscious choice to surrender control. Today, I release the grip of my expectations and embrace the uncertainty that life presents. In letting go, I find strength, resilience, and a profound sense of freedom. I trust that by relinquishing control, I open myself to new possibilities and allow the universe to guide me on a path filled with growth, joy, and serenity. This declaration is my commitment to surrendering, knowing that in surrender, I discover the true essence of living."

SELF-REFLECTION QUESTIONS

1. What would it feel like to release control and trust the process in areas where I currently resist it?

____

____

____

2. What fears or beliefs underlie my resistance to surrendering control?

____

____

____

3. What aspects of my life am I currently trying to control tightly?

____

____

____

PRAYER

I let go of my need for control and open my heart to the teachings that each moment has to offer. Give me the serenity to accept what I cannot change, the courage to change what I can, and the discernment to recognize the difference. Help me find calm in the face of uncertainty by guiding me through the twists and turns of life's river. You are with me, guiding me to my genuine and highest self. I find strength in surrender.
Amen.

Conclusion

As we close this 21-day journey, I want to recognize your devotion, boldness, and transparency. Each day, you have welcomed affirmations that challenged you to look within, face your anxieties, and appreciate your strengths. Remember, the power of affirmations lies not just in the words themselves but in the beliefs and actions they inspire in us.

This adventure marked the beginning, not an end. The seeds of change you have planted over these three weeks need nurturing to grow. Allow the knowledge you've obtained to serve as a guiding light for you. Continue to revisit these affirmations and let them evolve with you as you continue to mature and expand your horizons.

Personal growth is a lifelong journey, filled with both challenges and victories. Keep seeking out moments of reflection, keep setting intentions that align with your deepest values, and keep taking steps, even small ones, toward the life you envision for yourself.

Thank you for sharing this journey with me. May the affirmations shared become a foundation for your continuous growth, a source of strength in times of doubt, and a reminder of your limitless potential. Here's to moving forward, with hearts open and spirits high, ready to embrace the endless possibilities that lie ahead.

ABOUT THE AUTHOR

Angela Daniel is an inspiring new author based in Snellville, GA, whose passion for empowering women shines through her every word. As a certified Holistic Spiritual Life Coach and a licensed minister, Angela has devoted her life to supporting women in their journey toward healing and empowerment. Through her voice, teaching, and writing, she champions the use of affirmations as powerful tools for women to reaffirm their strength, resilience, and inherent worth.

Angela's work is deeply influenced by her holistic approach to life coaching and spiritual ministry, where she integrates affirmations into practices for overcoming life's setbacks. The affirmations she uses are vessels of empowerment, filled with actionable insights that guide women to transform their challenges into stepping stones for growth.

Angela's debut book is a reflection of her life's work and mission: to empower women to face life's adversities with courage and grace. Angela believes in the transformative power of affirmations to reshape thoughts, ignite positive change, and foster a deep sense of self-belief and inner peace.

Angela invites women from all levels of society to join her on this journey of self-discovery and transformation, reminding them that with the right affirmations, they can reclaim their narrative and emerge stronger than ever.

Made in the USA
Columbia, SC
03 April 2024